The Secrets to Unlocking Your

# Psychic Ability

# The Secrets to Unlocking Your

## *Psychic Ability*

## Matthew Fraser

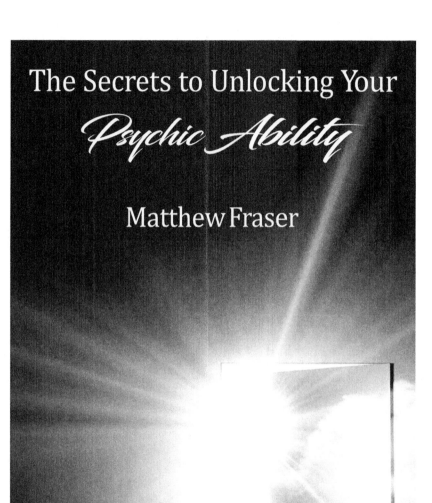

ISBN-13: 978-0-615-95965-8

# CONTENTS

# CHAPTER ONE:

## Growing Up Psychic

WHETHER WE REALIZE it or not, we all have the inner ability to find the answers we need to handle any given situation. Commonly referred to as being intuitive or psychic, this remarkable gift allows us to open our senses so we can hear, see, feel and understand on a deeper level the unexpected circumstances that surface in our lives. This ability will always be there to help us find comfort and light through any difficulty and provide the guidance needed to enrich our lives.

To help you to understand more about this skill, let me take you back to my life as a child. Growing up with a psychic mother and grandmother, it probably shouldn't have been a shock that I had inherited the family trait. However, when you're a little boy whose primary concern is whether he should choose chocolate or strawberry ice cream, voices calling your name in an empty room can be a most unwelcome surprise.

For a time, I was petrified to go to bed. Almost every night I would hear faint whispers enter my room with the ease of smoke under the door, building in intensity, swirling like leaves around me as the spirits of those who had passed vied for my attention.

Now, if one of them had said he was music icon Frank Sinatra, I might have risked a peek from under the covers, but no such luck.

My mother and grandmother did what they could to calm my fears. Little by little I came to expect, not necessarily accept, that I would have nighttime visitors. Eventually, the nights when no spirits came left me wondering what had happened, and if I had done something wrong. As my comfort level increased, so did the uninvited callers.

Soon I began seeing full body apparitions as though a real person was standing in my doorway. These appearances sparked a whole new level of concern and I recall how bedtime continued to raise the fear that I would be bombarded by passing spirits and those on the other side trying to talk to me. The strength of the visitations heightened to where even during the day I would see people who were in spirit flash before me or out of the corner of my eye. I was a child with a lot of unwanted "friends" I couldn't tell anyone about.

Every night I kept all the lights on in my bedroom and made my mom sit on the end of my bed until I fell asleep. It got to the point that I was so fearful and reluctant to embrace the ability I had, that I tried to shut it off completely when I entered middle school. I would not be back in touch with my abilities until later on in my teenage years.

My grandmother Mary grew up in a strict Catholic household where she wasn't allowed to mention or discuss any of the psychic experiences she would have as a child. Our childhoods paralleled in that she too heard and saw those who had departed, both in her house and also when she would visit family and friends. Because of her family, my grandmother kept these experiences hidden.

When my mother was born, she had the same gift. Mom grew up in a time where she too was afraid to talk about the abilities that she possessed with the outside world. In those days, this ability was kept very secret. My grandmother did readings for close friends and family in the privacy and safety of her home. It was something that was done in clandestine meetings and never talked about. To this day, my grandfather has no idea that this was going on in his own house! The readings were done while he was either out of the house or at work. Grandma never charged anyone. She felt her amazing gift should be used to help those in search of answers within their life.

I never truly knew or believed that I was psychic. It was always something that I had kept hidden from the outside world, afraid that others would not understand. Most of us have unsolved mysteries or watched TV shows with stories of those who had encounters with ghosts or apparitions, and I just hoped I was going through the same thing. Surrounded by a loving, psychic family, I finally realized that these incidents were much more than just odd coincidences or disturbances, and that I too had an incredible ability, a gift, that allowed me to see and hear those who had passed on.

Still, even while a youth, I always had an inner drive to help people. Early on I wanted a career in the medical field to help people who were sick. The summer before I entered college to fulfill my dream of being an EMT, I had an experience that reminded me of the ability that I had and forever would change my life.

A group of my friends had decided to visit a psychic to see what the future held for them before college. I went with them, without a clue I was in for a big surprise. I must explain here that prior to this event my beloved grandmother had passed away. The psychic not only knew that information, but said she had a message for me, courtesy of my grandmother.

According to the psychic, Grandmother Mary said I was to embrace the gift I thought I'd buried and use it to deliver messages from those who had passed into the spirit world to the loved ones they'd left behind. Needless to say, the goose pimples on my arms looked like a mountain range. I didn't know what to call the sensation at the time, but now I realize it was that moment of clarity when the door to your destiny opens and your life path stands before you, waiting for you to take the first step.

That night I went home and tried to use my abilities to connect with the other side as the psychic had told me. To my surprise, I was able to see and hear the same things I had experienced as a child. I heard whispers around me and my name being called. Images and visions flashed before me like pieces of a jigsaw puzzle inviting me to complete the picture. For the first time in my life, I truly was not afraid of my ability. I realized I had the ability to control what was happening and that the gift had never left me even though I had turned it off so many years prior. It was a huge transformation in my life; to embrace who I was meant to be. Soon after, I began to read for close friends and family. The first reading was for an aunt of mine looking to connect with an aunt of hers that had passed. As I closed my eyes I began to see images of dishes in a kitchen cabinet and a new rug being laid out on the floor. A second later I blurted out that her aunt wanted to say that she had seen the rug and dishes. I remember I had no clue what that meant, but tears of joy were streaming down my aunt's cheeks. She explained that before her aunt had passed she installed a new rug in her house as a surprise. Sadly, the aunt was never able to see it due to her illness. She discussed how she had recently taken the deceased aunt's dishes home to her house to display them in her kitchen cabinet. That experience instantly validated my ability to communicate with those who had passed on, and I've never questioned my gift since.

The next year I visited the college dorm room of a female friend. I immediately heard names spoken to me, identifying the potential boyfriends my friend would be introduced to during her semester at school. I told her she would meet three men who I described and named. That was the experience which demonstrated I could also see the future. Not long after that I received the call that she had met and became friends with all three.

During one college visit, I was standing in a dorm room, examining a wall collage of pictures. Without warning, one of the photographs, a middle aged man, spoke to me. He announced that he had passed and had been a second father to the girl residing in that room. Afterward, that girl walked in and verified that the picture was of her dad's best friend who had passed and had been a very influential and fatherly figure within her life.

What struck me odd was that I didn't find anything strange in the fact a photograph had carried on a conversation with me.

More and more experiences followed as I became more comfortable sharing messages from loved ones with their family members. I did pursue my dream and received my EMT certification in order to complete my goal of possessing the skill to help others. I later learned I could use both of these wonderful abilities to help those on both a physical and emotional level by passing on messages that would bring joy, comfort and closure to families, and also use my training as an EMT to aid those who were sick and in need of medical attention.

It has been an honor and a privilege to be able to use these gifts and pass on messages that bring closure and guidance to all those who need it. From being able to pass messages from those in spirit at live events, to being the guest speaker at benefits and keynote entertainment supporting charities, being able to show others that our loved ones never die and they are always around us is truly the gift that keeps on giving. These messages of love from those on the other side allow us all to have the comfort of knowing our loved ones are still with us, watching over us, smiling when we laugh, and sharing all the joyful moments that come our way. Messages of guidance and support come through to show us that there is peace at the end of the tunnel and can, on occasion, shine a light on the life road we all must to travel. Intuition is something we can experience to find the answers and guidance to help us overcome the many obstacles life places in out path.

# CHAPTER TWO:

## *What is Psychic Ability?*

MANY PEOPLE WONDER if they possess Psychic Abilities. Believe it or not, everyone is psychic to some extent. We all have the ability to tap into another vibration and gain access to universal information that will help guide us through life. I liken this ability to having a direct connection to heaven that allows us to see and hear visions of the past, present, and future and discover what secrets they hold. Some people even have the capacity to connect to a place I like to call "The Other Side." This is a place (often referred to as heaven) beyond the veil that we enter after our soul leaves the physical world. People who have this ability are able to connect with those who have passed on in order to receive and convey messages from the spirits of loved ones.

When we are born with this level of psychic ability, no matter how much we try to ignore it, it will keep coming back and pushing us to learn more about this gift. Education, the desire to expand our sphere of knowledge, is a powerful motivator in and of itself. Combine that yearning for education with psychic energy waiting to be released, and curiosity quickly turns to a need to learn more about ourselves.

So let's start our journey of discovery by defining "psychic ability?" Psychic ability is our mind and body's reading and acknowledging the energy and vibrations that surround us every day. This capacity exists in many different categories; from the traditional expectations of predicting the future to being intuitive (knowing) or even being a medium (speaking to the dead). Moments of connection with our inner skills may appear as a gut feeling about the future, premonitions through dreams, or seeing spirits walk through the house. Our psychic abilities differ from person to person. Each individual has been provided their own unique way to tap into their hidden power.

Psychic abilities are broken down into three basic categories: clairvoyance (Clear Seeing) which is the ability to see, clairsentience (Clear Sensing) which is the ability to feel, and claircognizance (Clear Knowing) which is the ability to know. We use all three of these capacities when performing a psychic reading or tapping into psychic vibration. Everyone has had at least one experience or encounter with one of these categories sometime in their life. Although all of us are able with the proper guidance to use all three of these senses, the average person will have just one that is their primary or strongest sense that will be utilized the most. While reading this book, readers may encounter a degree of comfort arise during our discussions of the various categories of psychic ability. This is the sense the individual uses, knowingly or unknowingly, in everyday life. Its familiarity to our mind and body is what provides the comfort. Let's take a look at some examples.

An artist may decide to focus on clairvoyance since that person already possesses a natural ability to see beyond the obvious and into what could be. A musician may want to work more with clairsentience as hearing is an integral part of their life. A business person may relate more with claircognizance as their mind is always at work, so the capacity of "knowing things" may come easier to them. See the connection? Take a minute to consider your everyday life, work, hobbies, etc., and see what category you might best fit into. While reading this book you may get a sense of all three categories, so don't worry if you can't willingly connect with one yet. Relax, sit back, and allow your familiar sense to step forward.

Let's discuss a few "common" occurrences of psychic ability.

We have all had that sensation where we say to ourselves, "I knew that was going to happen" or "I knew that." This inner voice that we either hear, feel, or just know comes from our psychic ability. I like to call this voice our "Spirit Guide," a person who has passed on and has been assigned to assist us when we open ourselves to the psychic world. Spirit Guides walk with us every day while we travel life's path. It is that guide we hear saying "go for it" or at other times sounding more like our mothers when they say, "That's not a good idea." Our guides are always looking over our shoulders, sending us signals. Granted, we don't always listen, and in those moments we usually end up wondering why we didn't listen. So, yes, as we will discuss, trust is an important aspect of this relationship.

Whether we know it or not, we are constantly tapping in and out of our psychic senses on a daily basis, picking up hints and clues to what is going to happen next, or even what the outcome will be of a certain situation. The more we begin to realize that we are receiving these psychic messages the more we open ourselves to a spiritual level and achieve greater clarity.

As I touched on a paragraph ago, one of the main obstacles we face when tapping in or using our abilities is doubt. We do not believe what we are hearing or seeing. We don't "trust." One of the things we must learn as we start to develop our gift is that often times we will be shown an occurrence or event in a vision or dream, and that same circumstance will present itself in the physical world. Without trust, we won't be prepared.

For example: We may be shown a place in a dream that we have never seen or visited, and then a few weeks later we arrive in that exact location in the physical world. If our presence there is pleasant, no worry. But if the experience is negative, we only have ourselves to blame for not being prepared. We didn't trust the information that had been provided to us. Trust can't be accomplished overnight. None of us would go out for an evening and leave our children with someone we hadn't previously established a level of comfort with. Building trust is a journey accomplished one step at a time.

Consider our spiritual journey as a flower about to bloom. The petals are closed tight. Slowly, the fragile flower begins to open, ending in a full reveal of the wondrous beauty hidden within. We all start off the same way, one step at a time, receiving bits of information here and there until we allow our minds to open up to all the senses.

One of the key things we can do to speed up this process is not to be afraid. Our abilities are a God-given gift, and as much a part of us as our heartbeats They are here to bring nothing but positive experiences into our life by empowering us to help ourselves and those around us with the privilege to decipher information that can provide guidance, comfort, or warning, if we only listen without fear.

With the gift of psychic ability, there are no boundaries; we can use our intuition to find out anything such as: Health Concerns, Business Deals, Love and Relationships. There is no question too big or too small. The more you use your gift, the more it will flourish and grow stronger. We should never be shy about testing our abilities. Here's a simple exercise to try when you're driving and can't find a parking space. Ask the guides in your head to help you find a parking space, and then clear your mind so you can "hear" the response. Wherever you feel drawn to, point the car in that direction. Odds are that you will see a parking spot waiting for you.

Once we are tapped in, our intuition and abilities will always be there when we need them. When we begin to feel comfortable in our abilities and start asking questions on a daily basis, we will see that after a while we don't even need to ask. No matter where we go we feel the energy around us. And eventually, we also feel the energy surrounding other people.

Always bear in mind that intuition is our higher self talking to us. While our mind is doing its job of keeping us on task, our higher self is engaged in sending us signals via intuition to keep us and those we love away from dangerous situations and getting us excited when it's time to move forward with new opportunities. The more we accept that our intuition is talking to us, the easier it will be to trust its message.

One of the primary ways to open up our psychic senses is by asking for signs. It doesn't matter if you are clairaudient, clairvoyant, or claircognizant, signs can be seen and recognized by everybody who is willing. For example: I had a client who came in for a session after going through a breakup with her boyfriend. She was very distraught and needed validation that the two of them were going to get back together, though I had already provided her with that information. I told her to go home and ask for signs.

The next morning the signs started bright and early. No matter where she turned, her boyfriend's first name was front and center: the morning news, a magazine in the dentist office, and even an article she was reading online where the columnist had the exact same name! Finally, she understood that their relationship was meant to be and no longer needed any extra validation. Once she acknowledged what her guides were trying to tell her, the signs of their relationship stopped because they weren't necessary any longer.

The point is, we can ask for signs regarding anything we want; what kind of work we should go into, if we will marry the person we're dating, or even whether a friend who is pregnant is having a boy or a girl. We can even ask a loved one to show or reveal a sign that they are around us in spirit. The possibilities are endless. All we have to do is ask.

Yet, while our gift's bounty is plentiful, it doesn't come with a fast forward button we can push to speed up the process. Patience is a virtue when it comes to psychic ability, and there isn't a shortcut or magic download that will configure awareness while we grab a tomato sandwich. We need to be focused and allow our skills to grow at their own pace. It's almost like learning a new language. What seem like obscure signs and symbols will take meaning when we begin to read and receive our clairvoyant messages.

I do at times recommend one time-proven suggestion that can help overcome the urge to rush this journey—meditation.

Meditation can be a huge asset when developing psychic ability. The spirit world is on a much different vibration than we are. Their vibration is very high, and the vibration in our physical world is very low.

Think of it this way; a helicopter blade spinning would represent the vibration energy of the spirit world and a ceiling fan would represent our vibration. Through meditation we can raise our vibration to a higher level so we can abut the spirit world. To put it in more everyday terms, our body and mind are like a cell phone: the more we use it, the more we drain the battery until we are unable to make calls. Our minds work the same way, the more we worry and stress, the more we cannot connect and receive messages. Meditation allows us to recharge our inner battery and wipe our minds free of the daily influx of clutter so we can focus on receiving messages and physically growing our mind.

A common misconception of meditation is that people often think or relate meditation with participants sitting cross legged in a room with their eyes closed. Meditation can take many forms and include just as many activities such as reading, walking, gardening, and, yes, even the traditional approach of sitting in a quiet room with your eyes closed. It comes down to whatever works for you. Whatever calms and puts your mind at ease is the approach that should be used. For me, reading a book on spirituality is my source of peace. Reading sends my mind into a positive state where I can escape reality and listen to my own thoughts while being surrounded by the positive reassuring words of a spiritual book. Many find that sitting in a room, listening to the soothing sounds of music helps take them away from the worries of society and everyday life. Others have discovered that walking through the woods, smelling the fresh air while surrounded by the bare necessities puts their mind at ease and allows stress to bleed into nothing.

I want to again emphasize that when you find the niche that works for you, use it! It may take a couple of tries, but when you do find it, you will know it. You will begin to see that no matter how busy you are or no matter what is on your mind, you can go into meditation and be carried away into another world of calm, reassuring energy. While reading this book, sit in a quiet place and let your mind soar to the other side. It just might be the start of your spiritual journey.

## Chapter 2 EXERCISE:

# Finding Your Ability

In this exercise we will explore what psychic ability you work closest with.

Read the scenario below and focus on how it plays out in your mind.

Do you see it or visualize it; hear it, feel it or sense it?

You are walking through a local park. You look down and see the soft green grass below your feet. You look up and see the cloudless sky, blue as can be, as the sun beats down on your face. Children are playing while their parents sit close by, listening to music from a portable CD player.

How did this scene play out in your mind?

Did you mainly see the park in front of you? *(Clairvoyance)* Did you feel the grass beneath your feet? *(Clairsentience)* Could you hear the children playing in the distance?

*(Clairaudience)*

Could you hear the music being played, and if so, what style was it? *(Clairaudience)*

Could you feel the sun on your face? *(Clairsentience)*

Could you see the faces of the parents and children, and the details of the scenery? *(Clairvoyance)*

What sense did you discover you used the most? The sense you used the most while considering the unfolding scene will be your strongest and will most likely be your primary psychic ability.

# CHAPTER THREE:

## *Tapping into Intuition*

INTUITION IS THE first sense we begin to become familiar with when we start to tap into our psychic abilities. I like to think of intuition as a super sense that allows us to feel on a deeper level. We all know that we have the five senses—hear, see, touch, smell, and taste. Intuition is our sixth sense that lives inside us constantly, sending out signals so we can see the reality of the situation in front of us. These signals can appear as a voice that you hear in your head telling you to move forward with an opportunity, or it can warn us by sending us nervous and anxious feelings when we need to proceed with caution. Ever get the feeling that someone is lying to you, or that someone is not trustworthy? That uneasy feeling comes from our intuition. It is always working in the background. For instance, someone may appear to be telling the truth or appear to be trustworthy, but our intuition will always show us that there is more than what meets the eye. You may be interviewing a person for a position in your company, and your first thoughts are that they are friendly, outgoing, and appear to be trustworthy. Everything seems great and they appear to be a good candidate for the position, although there is something that is telling you not to hire them; a feeling that throws you off. The signs can come in many different forms. You start to feel nervous and anxious around that person, you get a sick nervous feeling, or you start to feel on edge or get a headache. This is your intuition at work. Some people may even hear an inner voice telling them plain and simple: "don't do it."

The thing about our intuition is that it will continue to get stronger and stronger until you cannot ignore it anymore and have to respond. The moment you listen to your inner voice and make the right choice, the feelings go away and you start feeling like everything is back to normal. Women have long held claim to "knowing" when their husbands cheat. How? Their intuition kicks in and they start to feel that something is different in their relationship, and they begin their investigation to find out what is going on.

Intuition doesn't have to be a bad thing and more often than not our intuition is there encouraging us to move forward with opportunities that are presented to us from careers, to relationships, to family situations. Let's say you get a job offer. You may be nervous at first but your intuition kicks in and gives you the reassuring feeling that everything will be okay, and that pushes you to say "yes" and take the new job. Another example of how intuition can help you is when you lose something. How many times do you run around the house searching everywhere because you lost your car keys? Next time that happens take a step back and take a minute to tune in and "feel." Become in tune with your intuition. Do you sense you left the keys in your car? How about your coat pocket? Intuition is always at work zoning in and telling you where to find your keys.

From small things like lost items to complex issues, like deciding on a job offer, intuition is there and working to lead you through your feelings. Intuition is there to keep you safe and protect you and oftentimes will keep you out of harm's way. Have you ever heard a voice in your head say, "slow down!" or "change lanes!" and then a car skids in front of you or gets in an accident right where you were supposed to be. Aren't you glad you listened? What about when you are driving and you are lost and cannot find your way home? When you calm down and listen, your intuition becomes your own internal GPS guiding you to the right routes and roads to take you home safely.

The great thing about intuition is that you can use it when helping other people, such as friends and family when they are trying to make a decision within their life. Many of us have had a friend who calls and starts talking about a new person they met and started dating. Our friend is ecstatic over how great everything is going and what a wonderful time they are having together. On the outside we are happy and excited for them, congratulating them and sharing their enjoyment, but on the other hand we get the feeling that it will not last. Almost always, a week later we get the fateful call reporting the breakup we knew was inevitable.

But, the opposite holds true as well. Sometimes we 'know' a friend has found that forever love long before they do, and we get to sit back and contentedly nod when we hear of the upcoming nuptials.

Are you starting to see the connection and get a feeling for how this all works?

When you are channeling your psychic abilities and are not sure of what your other senses are telling you, such as if you're clairvoyant and cannot tell what is being shown to you, you can rely on your intuition to kick in and clear things up. Intuition is the backup system that is there working 24/7, that you can always depend on, and is usually not wrong.

Let's examine some real life examples of when intuition was able to be used and was correct.

One of the readings I will always remember is a woman who came to me, seeking guidance because she thought that her boyfriend was involved romantically with another woman. She was devastated and nervous when she called me; there was evidence that she had found, leading her to believe that her boyfriend was cheating, and that the relationship between her and him was over. No matter how hard she tried not to believe it, everything pointed that way; calls from mysterious numbers, women from work texting him, and even things in his house that were moved or changed since she last visited.

I too could see what she was talking about, and the images started flooding in of the calls and the texts and everything that had tipped her off. But . . . my intuition was sending me strong signals and making me feel that he was committed to their relationship. No matter how hard I tapped into my other senses, my intuition stood firm, telling me "no" and giving me the feeling of being sick to my stomach when I even began to think that her boyfriend may be cheating. I had no other choice than to listen and tell her that he loved her very much, and my intuition even made me feel that she was going to marry him!

When I had told her what I had seen and felt, there was no way she could make herself believe me. She asked over and over again, telling me what she had found and trying to convince me he was cheating. Her mind was racing, and though she wanted to believe what I was saying, she was unsure what to do. I assured her again that he was faithful, and I just had the feeling her relationship would flourish and continue.

Despite what I had told her, she still was not able to believe it and went to the point of hiring a private investigator to follow him. To her surprise, the investigator turned up nothing; her boyfriend was doing exactly what he told her—no lies or deceit.

This was just many of the scenarios where intuition did not fail me. On top of the good news that her new boyfriend was trustworthy, the two of them became closer than ever and their relationship took off. The next thing I knew they bought a house, got engaged, and he even took her on vacation! The both of them are doing fantastic and enjoying their new life together.

Another example that I can give you about how intuition can assist you while channeling psychic abilities came from one of my live events, and is personally one of my favorites. During one of my first events, I started reading for a family who I saw was planning a big family vacation. I kept seeing a cruise and Disney World and them going and having a really great time. When I asked if they knew what I was talking about they had said, "no." I stood there in astonishment as I kept seeing all things Mickey Mouse flashing before my eyes. I was lost for words, wondering how I could be wrong. I had no alternative but to turn to my intuition that was giving me the feeling I was right. I told the family that they would see what I was talking about in the future and for now to just rest on it and maybe it would make sense to them later. What else could I have done?

The next morning I woke up to an email stating the family had a huge cruise planned to Disney World over Christmas vacation. It was supposed to be a surprise, and the parents did not want their daughter, who had been sitting next to them during our conversation, to know. This just goes to show you when in doubt, listen to your intuition. It is the safety net that is there at all times and you can always use it to fall back on. So when you're feeling unsure of a situation or a vision that is presented to you in a reading, tune into your intuition and let it guide you from there.

## Chapter 3 EXERCISE:

# Testing Your Intuition

In this exercise you will be testing your intuition by learning to trust the feelings and emotions that you will be sensing. What you will need for this exercise is a magazine filled with interviews of people such as celebrities. A gossip magazine would be ideal since you will be picking up on the people inside.

To start, pick up the magazine, hold it in your hands, but do not open it. Later we will turn to page 16 to see who is on that page, but for now just hold the closed magazine in your hands.

Now think about the 16th page and get a feeling of who could be on it. You are not looking for specific names or details. I just want you to feel.

Ask yourself these questions:

1. Do you feel that it is a male or a female on the page?
2. What color hair does this person have?
3. What type of career are they in; Are they an actor, business person, or singer?
4. Do you feel that it is an advertisement or a column talking about an actual person?

5. What type of energy do you pick up? Is that person fun, outgoing, and spontaneous? Or, do you feel that they are serious, laid back and calm?

6. Now, open to page 16. What did you find? Was your intuition right?

If you don't get it the first time keep trying! You are just beginning, and you can try this with almost any magazine!

# CHAPTER FOUR:

## *Developing Clairvoyance*

EVER HAVE A vivid dream that you could have sworn was real? Ever see a scenario play out in your mind, and then it happens right in front of you? This is known as clairvoyance.

Much like the dreams that we have at night, clairvoyance allows our mind to enter a dreamlike state, allowing us to see visions and symbols that appear in our head as though there were a TV screen in front of our brain. With the ability of clairvoyance, we see visions of the past, present and future. Those who are clairvoyant usually see things in two ways; the first and most common being through visions. The second is the ability to receive premonitions through dreams at night. Clairvoyance is the primary capability I personally use when performing a psychic reading. Clairvoyance works like this: we both have two thought waves, our psychic thoughts and our normal everyday thoughts. Our psychic thoughts run parallel to our everyday thoughts. To access these psychic thoughts, we must first push aside our normal everyday thoughts so that we can see and download only our psychic thoughts and visions through divine guidance.

Divine guidance is help that we receive from our guides and the energy of the spiritual world around us to see these visions and symbols. It sounds complicated, but in fact it is simple. To break it down, what we are doing is clearing out our minds so that the only thoughts we receive and that are in our head are our psychic visions and premonitions. Meditation aids in bringing them into clear view. You will begin to see images, visions and symbols so you can channel your psychic energy and ability.

What you are going to do is to first sit in a quiet, dark room or your meditation place where you feel most relaxed. The key here is to not be distracted. Once in a nice quiet and comfortable position, close your eyes; we will soon begin to focus on something called the white light.

The "white light" is a pure energy often referred to as "the white light of Christ." It is used by many psychics both for protection while reading a client, and also to tap into a higher vibration so that you can begin to receive psychic visions.

Once you feel calm and relaxed, I want you to close your eyes and begin to focus on a soft white light in front of your face. Focus on this white light, allowing it to grow brighter and brighter until it slowly begins to pervade the room with an intensity that nearly blinds you. Let the light surround your body like a cloak. Keep quiet and stay focused on this light as it grows to its maximum brightness. During this process while you try to focus in on this white light, you will be bombarded with thoughts from your everyday life trying to enter your mind. This is normal. When this happens, and it will, remain focused, tuning into this white light. Keep pushing out all of your thoughts and worries until your head is clear and your mind is in a room with nothing but pure, bright, white light.

The hardest part of this meditation is dissolving your own thoughts, worries and stress so you may enter this space. Once you are there, you are golden. It may take several attempts to enter into this space or even to get yourself to the point where you can see the light in front of you. However, keep trying. Don't give up. Sometimes the process can take up to an hour to allow your thoughts to leave and this light to fill your mind. Again, this is normal. The longer you meditate, the deeper you become within yourself and closer to the vibration. Once you see nothing but this light all around you and your thoughts of everyday life have faded away, it is time for the next step.

Think about a situation that is occurring in your life that you need assistance with. Think about the situation and what you need answered over and over again until you begin to see visions, and symbols flash before you.

Don't stress and try to figure out what they mean; just watch and let the visions and symbols form in front of you. They may start off as blurred orbs floating aimlessly in your mind, or random images flashing very quickly. Concentrate and let them come into focus. After your meditation, grab a notebook and pencil and write down what you have seen and experienced. Some of the symbols and visions may be unclear as to what they mean, but write them down so that you do not forget. When you start to read clairvoyantly, oftentimes you will be shown symbols that represent a person's life. To me, when I give a reading, the symbols are oftentimes revealed to me as a jigsaw puzzle that I fit together as I go through the reading. I will give you some examples of what I mean by these symbols. However, keep in mind your experience and symbols will not be the same as mine.

Every psychic sees different symbols and interprets them in their own way. I will describe some examples of what I am talking about. When I see a wedding ring in front of me I know that the person I am reading for is married. When I see the separation of hands in front of me, I see that the person is divorced or just came out of a break up. These are just two of the symbols that appear for me when performing a reading for a client. As you continue channeling your psychic ability you will be seeing hundreds of your own symbols that you will learn and put a meaning to as you go on. These symbols will help you when you need guidance within your life. One of the stories I am going to share with you is one that I will never forget and is how I learned one of my first symbols for financial difficulty.

One day a women came in seeking guidance after hitting a rough point in her life. When I tapped in and closed my eyes, I immediately began to see money being flushed down the toilet. I had no idea what it meant. I first asked if she had been spending a lot of money, to which she had replied no. She told me that she had very little money and that her and her husband were going through bankruptcy. I immediately understood what I was being shown—my guides were indicating that she was in fact going through a bankruptcy.

Now when I read for a client I know when I see that symbol that my guides are trying to get through to me that the person I am reading for is going through a bankruptcy or severe financial distress. As you start to read for yourself you will also begin to see some of the same symbols in your readings and begin to figure out what each one means.

To me money being flushed down the toilet symbolizes bankruptcy or severe financial distress, but to you it could mean money being spent on bathroom repairs. The point is that these symbols will be unique and just for you, so you will need to figure them out yourself through trial and error. The more you ask questions about the situations in front of you, the more you will begin to understand what each symbol means. One of the stories that I will always remember from when I first started going public with my abilities was when I had a vision of my coworker. One night before I went to bed I laid down to relax, and my body soon entered a state of meditation to which I was shown my coworker and little baby legs wearing little construction boots walking across a coffee table. I had already figured out that anytime I had a vision of a baby it meant that the child would soon make its way to the physical world; in other words, the person would soon be having a baby. I quickly picked up the phone and called my coworker to tell him the news. Since the baby was wearing construction boots I felt that his wife would soon be having a baby boy.

Two weeks later my coworker received word his wife was in fact pregnant. A month or so later, an ultrasound confirmed they would be having a baby . . . girl. I stood in astonishment when he told me. I could not believe I was wrong. I was just starting out reading for other people, but still, how could I be so wrong? I went home and thought about it. And then it came to me; the construction boots symbolized that the baby was "under construction" and the boots would become my symbol meaning that the baby would come out of the blue as a surprise, since that couple was not trying to have a baby.

Since then I have figured out that my symbol for a baby boy or a baby girl is a blue ribbon, or a pink ribbon. That said, through this process of trial and error you too will learn the meanings of each symbol and start to learn this new language. One of the ways that you can speed up this process is by asking your guides to show you different symbols for different things. For example, ask your guides in your head to show you a playpen every time there is going to be news of a baby. This will come in handy if your son or daughter, or maybe even yourself, have been thinking about having a child. You will be surprised when that same symbol comes up again and again when you are reading a couple who are looking to start a family.

If you are having a hard time figuring out the meanings to the symbols you are seeing, come up with your own symbols that you want to be shown and the meanings associated with them. It will help you to quickly become proficient in your reading and finding guidance for yourself. If you are having trouble viewing these symbols in front of you, or difficulty in gaining access to the state of meditation, do not lose hope. There is an alternative to aid you in seeing these visions.

Tarot cards are the best tool to use when you start to develop your clairvoyance. What most people do not know about tarot cards is that you do not have to know the meanings of the cards to perform a reading. If tarot cards are used correctly, then each card should be able to trigger a psychic vision or thought within your mind.

Start by going to the store and picking up a tarot deck, or just a plain old deck of regular playing cards. My grandmother never owned tarot cards but could conduct card readings with standard playing cards. Use your intuition to select a deck that feels comfortable to you. The key is finding a deck that will speak to you and allow you to see visions. To read with a deck of cards, start by holding onto the deck. It is best to sit in a quiet room by yourself where you are not interrupted.

Begin by asking a question about your life or something you feel that you need answered, and then lay down five cards. To choose the cards, spread the deck out in front of you face down and use your intuition to guide you into selecting five cards that will answer the question for you. Repeat the question in your head that you want answered while you choose the cards that you feel drawn to. You can lay the cards down any way you wish. Use your intuition to choose what way feels most comfortable for you. Once the cards have been chosen, focus on the cards in front of you. What do you see? What do the colors represent to you? Does it look like the outcome of the situation will be good or bad? Do you see yourself struggling with this situation or do you see a successful outcome? If you asked about who you will be meeting in the future, do you see characteristics of that person in the cards? Do you see numbers that could represent a month in which you will meet that person? Remember what you are looking for are symbols and pictures that stand out in the cards or represent situations for you. For example, if you ask about how things will work out with the new person you have met and you see cards that represent fighting or struggles, then you should seek further guidance for yourself by pulling five more cards that show you how you can help the situation. Pull more cards if necessary to aid in disclosing how you can get closer and avoid fighting with this person. Lay the cards out. What do you see? Do the cards remind you of speed? Are you moving into the relationship too quickly? Do the cards represent lack of communication to you; do you have to start communicating more? How about distance? Does distance play a role in why you will struggle in the near future? Hopefully, you see what I am trying to get at—let the cards speak a story to you. Do not over think it, just let the things you see flow out. I'll bet your accuracy will surprise you.

One of the other ways that we can see clairvoyantly is by having premonition dreams. The same way that we see things through our meditation, we see the same through our dreams. Start by keeping a logbook next to your bed. When you wake up in the morning record your dreams into your logbook. At the end of each month go back and read through the entries. Pay attention to your dreams as they could either show you a situation before it happened, or they can show you symbols that represent the future. If you have dreamed a friend of yours holding a new born baby, then chances are your guides are informing you that your friend will soon find out she is pregnant. If you have a nightmare or a dream where you are scared or running, it could represent you going through a stressful time and that you need to relax and take more time for yourself instead of stressing out. Not all people have premonition dreams, but if you are one who does dream, make sure to record them so that you can understand what your guides and higher self are trying to speak to you.

## Chapter 4 EXERCISE:

# A Language through Symbols

In this exercise you will be creating a list of symbols that you will start using during your reading. We will begin by creating a list of basic symbols to get you started so you can have some basic information when starting a reading.

Remember to select symbols that you will remember and recognize, symbols that you will know what your guides are trying to tell you the minute you see them.

1. Choose a symbol for finding new love.
2. Choose a symbol for financial success.
3. Choose a symbol for a change in careers.
4. Choose a symbol for moving.
5. Choose a symbol that represents positive news ahead.
6. Choose a symbol that represents communication.
7. Choose a symbol that represents a "Yes" when asking a yes or no question.
8. Choose a symbol that represents a "No" when asking a yes or no question.
9. Choose a symbol that represents money.
10. Choose a symbol that represents change.

Remember this is just a simple list of basic symbols so that you can get an idea of what kind of definitions you should be associating with each symbol. Your list will grow and develop to be more in depth as you move forward and start readings.

# CHAPTER FIVE:

## *Sensing Clairsentience*

**W**AS THERE EVER a time when you stood next to a friend or a family member and sensed that something was wrong, but couldn't figure out what? You "felt" their nervousness and stress about a situation before they ever said anything. Well, if you have ever had an intense feeling come over you, or emotions that you felt were not your own, then chances are you are clairsentient.

The ability of being clairsentient walks hand in hand with being empathic. People with clairsentience "feel" a situation as opposed to hearing or seeing it. The difference between empathy and someone who is clairsentient is people who are empathetic pick up and hold on to another's pain and oftentimes have problems releasing it or letting it go. People who are clairsentient use their ability to sense the outcome of situations or to assist them when they need guidance within their life. I like to think that when you have this ability you are like a sponge soaking in all the emotions and energy around you as if they were your own.

Clairsentience works through our emotions. You start to experience and feel emotions, worries and concerns relating to different questions and situations. It doesn't have to be negative either. You can feel the emotions of being happy or excited when focusing in on a situation like a job opportunity that you feel is forthcoming. Many times, people who are clairsentient will be able to pick up on illnesses or health concerns and find solutions to fix them.

If you are not feeling good and do not know what is causing you to feel that way, turn to your clairsentience to help. Where does your clairsentience lead you? Do you feel a pressure in your head or a weird feeling in your stomach? Pay attention because your clairsentience will show you where in your body you need to focus. Maybe your clairsentience is leading you to your stomach to show you that something you ate or drank is causing you to feel this way. Maybe your clairsentience will lead you to your head because they are showing you it could be caused by depression. Wherever it is, they show you what is affected in your body, so listen and tap into your intuition to gain more information and find solutions.

You can also use this skill to help close friends and family members if it is within your comfort zone. Keep in mind the effects of having this ability are not permanent. Many times after you acknowledge what you are feeling and think about it, the feeling will go away so that you may pick up on other feelings around your life. The way people who are clairsentient read is completely through their emotions.

Although I am not fully empathetic when I read, oftentimes my clairsentience will kick in, especially if the person I am reading for is nervous. I always know when a client is extremely nervous because the second they sit in front of me or call on the phone I begin to feel as though I am having anxiety. I start to feel nervous, my heart races, and I begin to pick up what my client is feeling at that exact moment. You can use your clairsentience in a similar situation with your love life. Let's say you start dating a new person and you want to know how that person feels about you. You can tap into your clairsentience to feel how that person is feeling about you. People who are clairsentient are very in tune with their relationships because they are very sensitive and caring, and with this gift they are able to connect and understand their partner on a different level.

All you need to do is sit in a quiet place and close your eyes. Next, think about that person and ask yourself how that person feels about you. Continue to keep your eyes closed. What sensations flow through you? Are there butterflies in your stomach? Is your heart fluttering? Do you feel unsure or worried? Pay attention to the sensations engulfing you, as you may have started picking up on what your romantic partner is feeling at that moment. Maybe you feel your heart is fluttering because when he or she is with you or thinks about you they get butterflies in their stomach. Maybe you start to feel unsure or worried because that person just came out of a past relationship and is afraid to re-enter a new one.

You will soon notice that the emotions you have started feeling match up with the person you are thinking about. Many times we already know what that person is thinking, but we can always tap into our clairsentience for further validation.

Now let's try to ask something specific. Let's ask what will help to bring the two of you together more. Close your eyes and start asking yourself the question in your head. What did you feel and pick up on? Did you feel like your ears were buzzing? Maybe the two of you need to listen more to each other. Did you feel a calm feeling come over you? Maybe you need to take things slow and just spend time relaxing and talking with each other. Pay attention to the emotions you start to feel with each question. If you do not understand what you are feeling or the emotions that you are associated with asking the question, use your clairvoyance and intuition to help you figure it out. Many of the techniques we had to learn when putting meanings to the symbols in clairvoyance will be utilized when putting meanings to the emotions that arise.

Another wonderful thing about this ability is that it can also be used for married people who want to improve their relationship. If you feel as though your marriage is not as lively as it used to be, turn to your clairsentience to find out why. When you start to think about your marriage, do you feel sick or run down? Maybe your partner is feeling sick or has been in pain that he/she hasn't told you about, and that is affecting your relationship. Maybe you start to feel your head throbbing and realize that your partner has a lot of stress going on in his/her life with work. Now turn to your clairsentience and ask what you can do to get things back to normal within your relationship. Do you feel your legs start moving, do you feel like you should start taking walks together and bonding. Do you feel happy and full of laughter? Maybe your clairsentience is telling you that you should go out and have fun and relieve some of the stress that has built up. Do you feel sad or depressed? Maybe your partner is depressed and you should plan a weekend getaway or small vacation to cheer him/her up, or just spend extra time showing them extra attention and showing them that you love them. You can use your clairsentience for just about anything.

Let's look at another example. Let's say you are buying a house and are excited because you just placed an offer and are wondering if the homeowners will accept your offer. You can ask your clairsentience if the home owners will accept your offer. If you start to feel overwhelmed with emotions and feel happy and excited as though the offer went through, then you know that your clairsentience is showing you that the house will be yours. If you start to feel let down and disappointed then your clairsentience is showing you that chances are you will have to place another offer or look for another home.

You can use this same technique when asking if you will get the job or loan you applied for, or the application you sent into a school. Let's flip it around and say you are trying to sell your house and wondering what season it would sell. Tap into your clairsentience. Do you get a warm feeling like the sun is shining on your face? Maybe that means your house will sell during the summer months. Do you get a cold feeling like you need blankets? Maybe your clairsentience is showing you that your house will not sell until the winter. From relationships to situations going on in your life, you can use your clairsentience to feel out a situation and determine the outcome and find solutions.

One of the best things that having the ability of clairsentience brings is being able to sense danger ahead of time. This is something that you really need to trust and to listen to if you have this gift. Case in point: you are getting ready to go to a party you have been looking forward to all week long, and the day is finally here. You walk to your car, and then out of the blue, you are overwhelmed with an urge not to go. Sweat beads on your lip. Nervousness quivers your jaw. Worry and anxiety clench your hands. You listen and decide that you will stay home. Suddenly, like a choking smoke has lifted, all the fears and worries are gone. This is how you know that you made the correct decision. Listen to your clairsentience and always remember that it is at work sending you emotions and warning you of situations that could potentially be unsafe.

At times it can feel like our clairsentience is our guardian angel watching over us with a parent's concern, and stopping us from entering into a bad situation. You will also use this ability when you are trying to resolve and prevent fighting with family, friends, and your romantic partner. Remember that because you have this gift and are able to feel on a deeper level than most, you will have a clearer outlook on the situation because you can tap into the feelings of the other person and find out why they feel the way they do. Because of their innate ability to feel and sense, people who are clairsentient make great teachers and counselors. If you too are clairsentient and are torn about what career to go into, try one of these areas. You will find yourself to be so happy and privileged to be doing the work.

## Chapter 5 EXERCISE:

# Tools for Life

In this exercise you will be learning to recognize and put a meaning to the emotions and feelings that you sense and pick up while using clairsentience. What you will first need to do is find a recent picture of yourself. Study the photo with a skeptic's eye. Who is the person in your hand? What do you see in the shape of their brow, the curve of their lips, the smile in their eyes? How can he or she improve their life?

What emotions are you picking up on?

Do you sense that you are an overall happy person? Or do you have to work on creating more happiness within your life?

Do you sense that you are overall healthy? What do you sense can be done to improve your health?

Do you sense that your life is moving in the right direction?

What do you sense you should be doing at this point in time to keep you on the path to success?

Take a moment to write down your thoughts and feelings while answering each question. Use this to reflect and bring changes to your life for your highest and best good.

# CHAPTER SIX:

## Recognizing Claircognizance and Clairaudience

IMAGINE THAT YOU'RE home alone, watching TV, cleaning, or writing an email, and then, suddenly, someone calls your name. You get up to look or even answer back, but nobody is there—the whole house is empty. If you have ever had a startling experience like this then you have the gift of clairaudience. Those who are clairaudience are able to hear things that others cannot. It's not at all unusual for these people to hear their angels and guides speaking to them in their ear as if a friend where close by whispering a secret to them.

This voice can either come in the form of a family member or friend with whom you are close, or possibly even a tone similar to your own voice. In opposition to clairvoyance, clairaudience is the ability to hear the past, present and future instead of seeing it in front of you. When these premonitions are spoken to you, the words originate from your guides and angels, helping you to either find solutions or to see the outcome of difficult situations.

Clairaudience can work in many different ways. You may

clearly hear an answer when you tap in, such as hearing a yes or no being spoken to you, or you may hear the situation or the outcome of the situation taking place around you as if you were right there in the middle of it as the events unfold.

To tap into this ability, begin by sitting in a nice quiet room devoid of any distractions. We are going to walk through a simple meditation exercise to open up your ears. Close your eyes and take a minute to relax. Focus on the comfortable surface you are sitting on; allow all your stress to escape so your head is emptied of all your thoughts and worries and you see nothing but the darkness of your closed eyelids. Now focus on your ears and allow the tingling sensation to grow stronger and stronger until you can feel your ears vibrating or pulsating.

Start to imagine a ball of white light. Allow the light to grow brighter and stronger until it covers both of your ears. Drift a yes or no question across your mind. Turn your head to the side as though you were facing someone sitting next to you and ask the question aloud. Now, listen. What do you hear? Did you hear a yes or a no? If you did not hear it on the first attempt, try the exercise again. Keep in mind that it is important not to strain yourself trying to listen and allow the answer to just flow naturally. The last thing we want is for the exercise to become a source of stress; that would be self-defeating. Take it slow, and stay calm and relaxed.

Earlier, we discussed receiving premonitions with clairvoyance. Clairvoyance is the visual sense in which you may actually see a pink ribbon in front of you symbolizing that a baby is going to be born into the family. With clairaudience, you may hear a baby crying, symbolizing the same blessed event. But as with any sense, our psychic hearing can aid us at a time we need help.

As we talked about in the last chapter, your clairsentience can lead you out of danger or help to prevent you from being in a car accident by sending you overwhelming feelings and emotions to steer you away from entering your car and driving at that point in time. With your ability of clairaudience it too will lead you away from that same situation by allowing you to hear a car accident. You could be walking to your car, and out of nowhere you may hear brakes locking, tires grinding, or metal crushing—strong sounds that will catch your attention and convince you to wait a little while before going on that car ride.

When you're driving in the car you may hear, "Slow Down!" or "Switch Lanes" or even "Pay Attention!" This is your clairaudience hard at work. You see, our angels and guides are with us every step of the way as we walk through life. They are always trying to communicate with us to help us through the stressful situations of our lives. We just have to choose to listen. Remember, not only do we have the ability to hear our angels and guides, but we also have been blessed with being able to hear the thoughts of others. Yes, I'm serious, and hearing others' thoughts doesn't require some alien form of mind-melding that entails squeezing some poor soul's temples like a walnut in a pair of pliers.

Allow me to explain.

Have you ever just met someone for the first time and then after introducing yourself to them you knew what they were going to say before they even had the chance to open their mouth? This is your clairaudience at work tuning into those around you!

People who have this ability are usually very good listeners and most usually choose a career as social worker or law enforcement due to their amazing ability to pick up on what the person in front of them is thinking. People with this ability are great at being able to sort through the lies and uncover the truth.

For example; a police officer who is clairaudient, asks a shoplifting suspect if he or she (thieves come in all genders, so we don't want to be biased) stole clothing from a certain store. The individual looks at the police officer and swears that he or she did not steal anything and is not guilty. The officer "hears" the suspect's voice confessing and admitting that it was them who had stolen the clothing.

Of course, the police officer actually hears what the person really said aloud, but his clairaudience was in the background sifting the lies to deliver the truth. You still have doubts? Didn't you ever wonder how your mom always knew when you were lying, even after you'd repeatedly rehearsed your claims of innocence and pulled every heartstring within reach? Believe me, moms know . . . pretty much everything we do. However, that motherly knowledge could very well have been her clairaudience speaking to her and shredding your lies. Oftentimes in a situation like this our clairaudience will talk to us in our own voice so we don't really know that it is our ability in action, leaving us to mistakenly believe that what we heard was just a "feeling."

Clairaudience also works very well when dealing with relationship issues. With our clairaudience at work, we are able to listen more carefully to our romantic partner and understand them on a deeper level. Consider the situation of being on a first date at a local bar. The person you are with may ask you to take a walk with them because they left something in their car. Your clairaudience comes into play and tells you that the person just wanted to sweep you away from bar so that they can talk to you alone and get to know you better. This allows you to understand that the person you are with does like you and wants to spend time alone with you talking and getting closer to you. However, while that example is a positive one, bear in mind that if you hear, "Stop! Don't go!" you should take that warning to heart. Our psychic senses are there to help and protect us. When they say, "Danger!" . . . listen and act accordingly.

Let's take a look at another real life situation. You have just started dating a new person and things are going very well. You are excited for your next date with that person. You go out and have a great time, but to your surprise your date ends things abruptly and decided to drop you off at home because they were not feeling good. Most people would think that their date is lying and that they blew them off. However, in this case your clairaudience assures you that he or she is indeed sick and needs to go home. The next week that same person asks you out again and you agree, the end result being you have a really great time. You realize that your clairaudience was right on target showing you that they were not lying to you.

Married couples and monogamous relationships can employ clairaudience to their benefits too. How about a case where a romantic partner is being recognized for an award at work and the event will be held the same day and time that you are scheduled to attend an outdoor concert with your friends. Your partner assures you that it is okay if you miss the award ceremony, as you did have the plans for a night out with your friends first. What an understanding sweetie, huh? Maybe, maybe not. Maybe your partner was placing what he or she thought were your needs over their own, and all isn't fine on the home front.

Then your clairaudience tunes in and you "hear" that your partner really wants . . . needs . . . you to be at his or her side and will be heartsick if you choose to miss the awards ceremony. Obviously, well, hopefully, you decide to attend the awards ceremony and everything works out in the end thanks to your clairaudience at work.

So, what did you hear that made you go?

Maybe you heard your partner's voice saying, "I wish you would be here" or "Please come." You might have even heard the applause as the award was delivered.

No matter what or how you hear the message, know that it is your clairaudience speaking to you, revealing what to do in that situation. You can ask for guidance in any environment at any time. Clairaudience is most effective when asking basic yes or no questions.

Switching gears slightly, but in the same category, claircognizance is the ability to "just know" information as though it had already been told to you. A fairly common example of this sense is when you are sick and in the hospital. You "know" that you have bronchitis long before the doctor runs any tests or retrieves blood work. Claircognizance is that first thought entering your mind and showing you the answer.

Many times we tend not to trust this sense, preferring to

overthink and analyze data that will eventually confirm the answer or response we had already been provided. Do you ever say to yourself "I knew I should have done that" or "I knew I should have gone"? That is us realizing we didn't listen to the message our claircognizance had provided. Another instance of this is when we meet someone for the first time and know that they are pregnant, or that they have children, or are married before they even tell you. You don't hear or see anything; you just "know" as if they had already told you this information in the past. Our claircognizance pops up all the time no matter where we go.

Sometimes it is so second nature that we don't even know we have the ability or that it is working for our benefit. It is very similar to our first instinct presenting itself in almost every single situation. It can present itself as our knowing how a person will react before they do, or understanding how a situation will unfold before the first domino falls. To provide a little imagery, imagine you walk into a grocery store and every shelf contains the same can of information, waiting for you to pick it up. Claircognizance almost feels like the information has just been sitting there in your head waiting for you to validate it.

The best way to develop your claircognizance is by accepting that it exists and trusting that it will manifest within your first instincts. Once you begin to realize that it is there, you can see how to use this skill and the accuracy contained within this intriguing sense. All you have to do is trust the information and run with it.

## Chapter 6 EXERCISE:

# *Developing Your Clairaudience*

In this exercise we will be learning how to develop our clairaudience so we may "hear" more clearly. Below are a couple of different scenarios. As you read each one, listen and record on a separate piece of paper the sounds that you hear as you visualize the descriptions.

1. You are sitting on the beach, watching ocean waves crash against a reef as high tide starts to roll in. Seagulls' shadows race over the sand. You drift your gaze to the sky and see the white birds with their yellow bills gliding above you in the heat of the sun. Looking, you notice a few children building sand castles while others run up and down the beach. Now, write down what you heard.

   What noise did the waves make crashing against the rocks? Did the seagulls squawk?

   Did the children holler or laugh as they play in the sand?

2. You are sitting in the bleachers of a football stadium before kickoff. Suddenly, the crowd yells and screams with excitement. You look down and see vendors hawking food to the hungry fans. Standing in front of a wooden bench,

a coach studies his playbook in preparation for the big game. The marching band gathers in the end zone.

What were the fans yelling and screaming?

What foods or drinks were the vendors shouting out?

Did you hear the sports announcer over the loud speaker?

Were the band members testing their instruments? If so, what were they playing, or what instruments were the loudest?

This week as you read news articles and magazines, listen and see what you hear while reading them. It will help you to tune yourself into your clairaudience and strengthen your ability.

# CHAPTER SEVEN:

## *Mediumship and Spirit Communication*

**F**AMILY MEMBERS WHO have passed away, never truly leave us. When we think about them, cherishing the moments that we have shared with them, they are there right beside us. We bring our loved ones with us no matter where we go; the tie of love that we share with them is never broken. When a family member or friend leaves us they move on to a place that I have come to know and recognize as "The Other Side," commonly referred to as heaven. It is a place beyond the veil that is the ultimate paradise where all our friends and love ones enter after they pass, where they are all together and are able to watch over us as we take our journey through life. The good news is that we can contact and speak to our loved ones beyond death's veil.

This form of communication is known as mediumship, the ability to communicate and receive messages from those who are in spirit after leaving the physical world. We have all had an experience where we felt a loved one in spirit around us. Time and time again you hear stories of people dreaming of their departed loved ones, receiving a sign from that person, or even seeing that person's spirit appear in front of them. This is validation that our loved ones are always standing by us, sending us signals and signs from heaven.

The signs can come in many different ways. It could be a song that comes on, a wisp of cologne as you walk down the street, or an object that awakens a memory. Have you even been in a mall or a public place and see a person walk by that looks just like a loved one who is passed? Guess what? That's your loved one in spirit opening your eyes at that exact point in time to show you that they are okay and to say hello. So how can you open up your senses so that you can hear, see and feel your loved one in spirit? If you haven't guessed it yet, the keyword is meditation.

Now that you have learned to develop all of your psychic senses: clairvoyance, clairsentience, claircognizance, you can now learn to develop mediumship to contact your loved ones on the other side. Mediumship requires the interaction of the other three psychic senses. You will use your clairvoyance to see your loved on in spirit, clairsentience to feel them, and clairaudience to listen to the messages that they have for you.

In this practical meditation you will allow your loved one to come in for a visit so you can reconnect with them and share in the joy of knowing that they are safe and at peace.

Begin as we have previously discussed by sitting in a comfortable, quiet place devoid of any distractions, noise or other people. Close your eyes and focus on the white light which should appear much quicker than when we first started these exercises. Mentally will your stress, worries, and thoughts to drain from your mind as you enter a place filled with loving warmth. Welcome the white light as it surrounds you and grows brighter and brighter until you are sitting in a room filled with nothing but white light. This is when we invite our loved one into our consciousness.

Let the name of that loved one fill your mind. Keep focusing until a blurry figure starts to form in the distance. Lock your mind's eye on that blurred silhouette as it moves toward you ever so slowly and forms into the loved one that you lost. Watch the facial features emerge. See the face of your loved one looking straight at you, happy and content, waiting to share with you a message that they have since wanted to tell you. Use your clairsentience to feel your loved ones presence directly in front of you. Embrace the warm, loving energy as it envelops you and your heart expands with the joy. Open your ears to the message your loved one carries with them. Tune in your clairaudience and listen to what is being conveyed. Hear the voice of your loved one whisper the words they have brought only for you. Remember the message as you allow them to slowly backaway and fade into the light. Allow the white around you to dissipate as you return from this wonderful meditative space back into your body.

Take a deep breath or twelve as you decipher the gift given you.

What did your loved one have to share that brought them from the other side? Did they speak to you about one of the favorite moments that they once shared with you? Did they offer advice about the future? Did they thank you for taking care of them when they were very ill? Did they whisper, "I love you"? No matter how big or small the message, rejoice in the knowledge that you were able to connect with your loved one. It's possible you feel a degree of despondency that your loved one has left again. But here's the real gift in honing your psychic skills: You can connect with them whenever you like or as often as you like, and your loved ones will always respond.

If you found it hard connecting or visualizing on the mediumship level, do not worry. You can always try again or repeat the meditation while only focusing on your strongest ability, whether it be just seeing them, hearing them, or feeling them. No ability is better or stronger than the other; you can use your clairaudience to hear them, clairvoyance to see them, or clairsentience to feel them. Whatever ability you find is the strongest, go back and meditate while using that ability to receive a message from the other side. If you are still finding it hard to connect, ask for signs from that loved one while you are waiting to further develop your abilities.

Signs are one of the best solutions to knowing and seeing your loved one's presence in everyday life. Whether it be driving in the car and you see their name on a license plate, whether it be at the doctor's office and a patient is called in with the same name or who looks like your loved one, the signs are all around us. All we need do is ask, and then sit back and watch our loved ones reach out to us.

One of the other things that you can do to hear from your loved ones in spirit is to ask for them to visit you in a dream. Dreams provide gentle vibrations for spirits to travel in order to visit because we are already in a calm, meditative state. If you wish to have the experience of dreaming about your loved one, ask for them to enter your dream before you go to bed. As you lie in your bed, think of your loved one and the memories you hold close to your heart. Think about them, tell them that you would love to hear from them and ask them to visit you in your dreams that night and to pass on any messages they may have.

The thing about dreams is that our departed loved ones do come to see us more often than not, in our dreams. Dreams are the perfect conduit due to our relaxed state.

Spirits may appear in the same form they possessed before they had passed, or they may appear younger or the way that they wish to be remembered. No matter what form they present themselves in, know that it is them coming toward you to remind you that they have never left you.

The thing about seeing our loved ones in dreams is that they will not come all the time. You see, our loved ones want us to enjoy our life. They do not want us to cry or grieve or stop living our life because of their passing. Because of this, they only come to visit us once in a while in our dreams, generally when we need them the most. Spirits may come during a stressful time when we need their advice, or at a time when you miss them and need to hear from them. One thing is certain; they want you to know that when they come to visit you in a dream it is really them. It is not just a coincidence or wishful thinking; it is your loved one trying to reach out and say hello. These visitations are very special and unique and should be held close to your heart.

Many times our loved ones will come when there is a new baby being born into the family. Our loved ones in spirit will be present at the time the baby is being delivered, handing the infant to our world as it is being born. More often than not during my career I have heard stories of people who have had dreams of their loved ones with a baby in their arms and then find out that their son or daughter is pregnant. This happens all the time. It gives us the validation of knowing both that our children or family member is having a baby, but also having the reassurance of knowing that our loved one is there, seeing and holding that same baby in spirit before it is born into the physical world.

One of the best ways to strengthen the communication between you and your loved ones in spirit is to talk to them. When you miss them and think about them, just start talking to them. The act may seem simplistic, and it should be. Say "hello," ask them a question or just tell them about your day. The more you talk to them either out loud or in your head, you open the communication lines between you and that person so the next time you have a question or need guidance you know that you can always turn to your loved one's spirit for help.

I am frequently asked why our loved ones do not appear to us as an apparition or in full body form. There are two answers to this.

The first is that it takes a lot of energy for your loved one to do that and the second reason is because they do not want you to be frightened, confused or to attempt to hold on to them. They want you to enjoy your life and to move on from their passing. If you ever need to feel closer to a loved one who is passed, hold onto a picture or an object that was once theirs. Feel their warm loving energy as you think about them and allow their peaceful energy to surround you. Clairsentience and intuition will enable you to feel their presence and recognize that they are present in spirit and sharing this moment with you.

The bottom line is, our loved ones are there at all times, watching everything that goes on in our families, watching our children grow, and enjoying the happiness we find in living.

## Chapter 7 EXERCISE:

# *Seeing Signs*

In this exercise we will be working on opening our awareness and awakening our senses to the signs that surround us. It may seem simple, but signs are the start to recognizing that seeing is believing. Begin by meditating, then select a loved one, either a friend or a family member, who has passed and ask them to give you a sign that they are near. Be specific and ask them to show you something that you would recognize right away; something that will absolutely have you convinced that it is them. Now, sit back, watch, and observe as signs can come in many shapes and sizes:

Did you smell a familiar scent around you that reminded you of that person?

*Example:* Cigar smoke, laundry detergent, cologne.

Did you see that person's name while you were out?

*Example:* Street sign with person's name, met a man/woman with the same name.

Seeing someone that resembled that person in spirit.

*Example:* Man on a bench resembling your grandfather, woman gardening reminding you of your mom.

Observing something that the person in spirit once loved.

*Example:* A dozen red roses, their favorite dessert, or a movie they could recite verbatim.

Did you hear a song that the person always sang along to when it came on the radio?

Signs can arrive in any shape or form. These are just a few examples to get your mind going and show you some of the most common reveals to watch for. The signs you receive will be specific and bring validation of a spirit's presence.

# CHAPTER EIGHT:

## Understanding Spirit Guides and Guardian Angels

In the corner of your eye a shadow moves. A feeling of being watched overwhelms you. No, you weren't dropped into a horror movie. Chances are you were seeing and sensing your spirit guide.

Spirit guides are assigned to us when we are born; they stand by our side and walk with us through our life journey, and give us strength and assurance when it's our time to pass to the other side.

It's not unusual for spirit guides to be confused with guardian angels or a family member who has passed. However, the three are completely different. A spirit guide is neither a family member nor a guardian angel, but a spirit whose mission is to keep us on track. We never met them in life. They were taught and given information on our whole life before we were born so that they may help and lead us as we enter this world.

If you ever had an imaginary friend as a child growing up, odds are you were playing and talking to your spirit guide. Most people have two or more spirit guides assigned to watch over their career, love life, health and more.

Have you ever had road blocks thrown in your way? Ever feel like one thing after another went wrong? Most times it was your spirit guide closing the doors around you until you finally found the one that would lead you on your path to success—the one you were supposed to be on. It can seem like our spirit guides have your daily itineraries already in their hand, and it's their responsibility to ensure we arrive on time to each appointment and make the proper turn at each crossroad. They follow us around like spy satellites, watching our every move, removing obstructions on the correct path, and planting immovable obstacles on the wrong route. When you enter this world our names have already been written on certain "gifts" that we are meant to have in our lifetime. Careers, future partners, the houses we live in have had your name on them all along. These gifts are individually specific and can only be claimed by the person they were designed for, and nobody else. It is up to our spirit guide to see that each gift can be delivered into our lives so that we keep moving forward on our journey.

Like a mother's love, our spirit guide is always there, always listening. The next time you feel like things are not going right or that the opportunities around you are fading into oblivion, turn to your spirit guide for guidance and direction. You can always ask them to open the doors that you are supposed to walk through and to lead you to the perfect road to find success. When you feel stuck, talk to them and then keep your eyes open for the path they will be sending you on.

So, what do your spirit guides look like? What are their names? Where were they or who were they before they came back in spirit to help guide you? All great questions, and we'll answer all of them.

What we are going to do in this chapter is meet and talk to our spirit guides. Later, we will meet and discuss our angels. Naturally, to do these things requires us to employ the psychic abilities we developed earlier. Sit in a nice quiet room away from any distractions. That's right, I want you to meditate. Use your clairvoyance by surrounding yourself in white light and ask that your spirit guide move toward you. Just as you had seen in mediumship, two blurred objects appear in the distance, slowly coming forward and taking human shape. Watch as your guides come closer into view and reveal themselves.

Guides do not look the same. They are as individual as the living person they serve. Get familiar with them. They won't mind. Are your guides men, women or both a man and a woman? Can you make out their facial features? What kind of clothing are they wearing? Use your clairsentience to get a feel for who your guides are.

The dispositions of spirit guides can be diverse. Do you feel that they are more serious? Do you feel as though they are motherly or nurturing? Do you feel as though one is nurturing and one is serious?

Next we are going to ask them their names. Concentrate on the images of your guides. When it feels right to you, turn to each one and ask their name. Have no worries, they'll answer.

Once you know their names you can ask them anything you want or call upon them at any time. Take a minute to tap into your intuition. Intuition can reveal what your guides have planned for you; should you stay in the same job or are you destined to pursue a new career? Are you going to stay in the same house, or is the home with the fenced-in yard you always dreamed of waiting for you? Will your finances straighten out, or should you make an appointment with a bankruptcy attorney? Let's certainly hope that's not the case.

My point is, take a minute to get a feel for what road you should be on. Whenever you have a question about the path you should take or the decision you should make, your guides will be right there laying out the path for you to travel.

When you have a question or need answers within your life, another source you can rely on are your angels. No matter who we are or what religion we follow, we all have angels around us, walking with us through our life here on Earth. Angels are magnificent, positive beings that come directly from the higher realm. They are here to watch over and protect us. Angels are constantly busy helping us through emotional struggles and showing us the positive, the brighter side to life.

Your angels can help you in so many ways. When you are sick, in danger, or need emotional support, your angels will lend a helping hand. Have you ever felt like you have avoided a dangerous situation just in the nick of time, had a serious accident where you could have died or been permanently injured, and you walked away without a scratch? Those are your angels protecting you as best they can as you walk through the physical world. Angels can be called upon at any given moment when you need assistance in getting through emotional or stressful times. That is what they are there for.

Angels come directly from God and are filled with nothing but love light and positive energy. They do not want to see you cry or be upset or go through an emotional time. They want nothing more than for you to be happy and healthy and enjoying your life. When you are feeling negative, tired or stressed, call upon your angels to help. They will absorb all the negatives invading your life, leaving you refreshed and rejuvenated. When depression overpowers you, call in your angels, and ask them to take it away.

Lie down on a nice comfortable surface, whether it is in the backyard on the grass, the couch in your living room, or on your bed, and start to envision your companion angels. Watch them as they come forward with buckets, fill them with the negative emotions that you have been feeling and carry them away leaving you with nothing but calm, positive, reassuring thoughts.

As far as your angels are concerned, you are the most important person in this world. Their goal is to take care of you and shed light on every situation in your life. It doesn't matter if you are having a feud with family members, close friends, or spouse, your angels will be there right beside you. Angels see tomorrow so much more clearly than we see today, so when you are unsure in a situation, call on your angels for emotional support. Everyone has at least two angels that stay with them to watch over their charge at all times.

Let's meet your angels so you can become familiar with their presence and identities. Just like we did when we met our spirit guides, we are going to do the same when we meet our angels.

Close your eyes and tap into your clairvoyance. Call upon the white light to engulf you and cleanse your mind and body of all negativity. Ask your angels to step forward into the light so that you can meet them. As they take form in front of you, take a moment to enjoy how magnificent they are. From their soaring wings, to their glowing skin, it's okay to bask in their beauty. Next, use your clairsentience to feel their energy.

Start to feel the nurturing, positive vibrations they emit and revel in the tingling that happens in your body as they approach you. Next, when it feels comfortable, turn to each angel and, using your clairaudience, ask each one their name.

Remember the names that you have heard and write them down so you do not forget them. Now, with the use of your intuition, ask your angels what you can do to bring you joy, happiness, and comfort in your life. Do they respond by showing you taking more time for yourself where you can enjoy the outdoors? Or, could it be a Caribbean cruise, or biking through the mountains?

Do they show you going back to school to enter the career path you dreamed of as a child? Or do they reveal you going away with your romantic partner on a vacation to reconnect and enjoy the relationship and closeness that you once shared? Between your guides and angels, you should never feel helpless or alone because they work as a team. All that company might make an elevator ride feel a little crowded, but you will never, ever be alone.

Your guides show you the direction and the path you need to take while your angels provide you with the love, comfort and support that you need along the way. You can always ask your angels to calm you down before a job interview, to wipe away your emotions before meeting with a client, or even to help you in settling a dispute between you and your friends. Your angels will always back you up when you need them. You have but to reach out to them for assistance.

## Chapter 8 EXERCISE:

# Calling in Your Angels

In this exercise we will be calling in our team of angels to help give us a quick pick me up and take away all past emotions of feeling, hurt, neglect or stress. We will call upon the angels to free us of any emotional pain or suffering that we may be holding onto from the past.

Take a moment to sit down and relax, close your eyes and think about all the heavy burdens, grief and pain that you have once experienced in your life. Think of all those burdens and emotions as words on a chalk board. Envision how nice it would feel if each word was erased and disappeared from your life.

Call in all your angels. Watch as they each take a word and erase it from the board. Continue watching until there are no more words to erase. All you are left with is the positive reassuring energy of the angels that are with you, standing by and comforting you.

Take a moment to write down on a separate piece of paper how you feel now that each burden has been lifted and all past emotions have been erased and replaced with positive, loving energy and thoughts. What do you have planned for yourself now that these past emotions have been erased?

# CHAPTER NINE:

## Putting Together your Senses

Now that we have learned how to tap into each of our abilities, we can use each skill to find guidance or solutions in any situation. No matter what difficulty stands in our way, we can call upon our newfound abilities to help locate a positive outcome or solution. The psychic senses we have learned about and developed will intertwine and work together to provide the answers we need.

Let's take a look again at some examples of situations that you may encounter so you may see how each ability can assist you with finding mental clarity, ease your stress, and also assist you in finding a positive outcome.

The number one topic that invariably receives the greatest number of questions is love and relationships. So, let's explore a scenario in which you went out on date and met a seemingly really great person. The two of you connected on a variety of emotional levels and the future appears bright. The two of you go on multiple dates, take day trips and even introduce each other to your friends. What could go wrong?

Naturally, a lot could and will go wrong or there'd be no point to this example.

The blossoming relationship, on the surface, appears to be one that was "just meant to be." Then the rainbow turns black. Out of nowhere your romantic partner announces he or she "cannot commit to a relationship at this time." You are heartbroken—devastated. However, you have an edge, a whole card you can play at any moment you choose. Withdrawing on your psychic abilities, you decide to tap in and find out what is really going on.

You first start by calling in your angels to assist you with the emotional distress weighing you down. Your angels take away all the tears, worries, anger or grief, replacing those unwanted negatives with calm clarity. The next step is to rely on intuition.

You ask your intuition if the relationship is truly over, or if you will be able to have another chance with this person, and your intuition right away tells you, yes, you will be with this person in the future.

Next, you tap into clairvoyance so you can "see" what affected the love interest's decision to end the relationship and discover what he is going through. The puzzle pieces immediately fall into place. Unpaid bills are piled on a desk. An elderly man in a hospital bed materializes in your mind's eye. Your love interest is seated at his side, holding the older man's hand, wiping his sweaty brow. The man in the bed is his father, and is very ill.

It's only human to feel a sense of relief that stress and worry caused the breakup—not something you did or caused or could have prevented. Claircognizance kicks in and reminds you that you know that your partner is a very nervous person and all this stress is wearing on them physically as well as emotionally. Your clairsentience overwhelms you with emotion and makes you feel as though that person wants to be in a relationship although they are smothered by the stress and feel as though the relationship will suffer because of it. You tune into your clairaudience and hear that you need to be patient and not add to the strain.

Lastly, you call in your angels and guides and ask them for advice regarding this. They confirm your intuition by showing you that in the future you will be with this person again, but right now your need to bring yourself back to the basics and be the supportive friend your love interest truly requires right now. You may feel as though you need to go back and reestablish that friendship and a trust bond between you and this person if the relationship had moved so fast you didn't get to establish that support and trust. Your guides and angels show you that once you pick up the pieces and get that support and friendship in place by helping that person through this difficult time, you will later be able to move forward and build a future from the foundation being laid one brick at a time.

Do you see how all your senses come together when you need them? It's almost like the abilities partner with each other to paint a vivid picture in your mind of the situation as it really is, and the inevitable outcome.

Ready for another scenario?

This time, let's pretend that you are not feeling well and you are not sure if you should go to the doctor. Your intuition gives you a gut feeling that you should get yourself checked out, but for whatever reason, you are still not sure. You decide to keeping looking into your sickness by turning to your clairvoyance to see if you can pinpoint exactly what is wrong.

You tune into your clairvoyance and see a blood pressure cuff. This sign probably indicates you may have a problem with blood pressure, but you still are not sure if the blood pressure cuff symbolizes that your blood pressure is high or if it's just you seeing that you need to visit a doctor.

Being the stubborn type, you next turn to your clairsentience and you sense that you should just suck it up and go to the doctor. Still, you turn to your claircognizance which helps you to remember that you do have a blood pressure problem and it would be best if you got your butt to a doctor. Then your clairaudience kicks in and sends the sound of your heartbeat in your ears. Last, but not least, you turn to your angels and guides who tell you it's time to quit messing around and get to a doctor. As encouragement to make the right decision, they envelop you with the warm, comforting feeling that if you will put your shoes on and get to the clinic, everything will be all right. So, after turning to all your psychic abilities, you decide to go to the doctor and discover that indeed your blood pressure is high. A change in medication was all that was required to remedy the problem.

Whenever you are in doubt, you have your psychic abilities present to help you get on track and lead you in the right direction. However, and I can't understate this, trusting your abilities is key. When your health is the issue, listen to that first voice telling you to seek medical help.

Let's take a look at yet another example; one a tad less life-threatening. You have been thinking about moving and have no idea why. Moving has been on your mind for about a year now and your intuition tells you that by the end of this year you will be living in a different home. You turn to your clairvoyance and begin to see this new house. It is medium sized, has a big backyard with a pool, and a lovely porch where you can sit outside and read or have friends over on your days off.

Clairsentience overwhelms you with emotions as though the move has already happened and showing you that you will be very happy and excited in the new house. Claircognizance reveals that you will indeed be moving and confirms your intuition by bestowing the knowledge that the move is right around the corner.

Clairaudience sends the number $130,000, which happens to be an amount you can afford.

Finally, you ask your guides and angels for their input, and they show you that this new house will bring you lots of happiness and joy. They lift the curtains of doubt to unveil that the new house will be everything you have ever wanted; the right price, the right amount of rooms, and the perfect location. Excitement fills the air, and your guides and angels celebrate the impending move with you.

Everything we have discussed is only the start of your spiritual journey. Now that you have learned how to tap in and use your psychic abilities and senses, you can call on them to provide the guidance, direction and comfort you need at all times. Your abilities will never leave you. The more you utilize them, the stronger they will become, allowing you to see more, feel more, and to sense more. You will be able to use these abilities as a tool to unlock a life filled with joy, happiness, comfort and understanding.

The best part of being a psychic medium is being able to meet and connect with wonderful people.

Thank you so very much for spending some time with me, and please let me know what you thought of *The Secrets to Unlocking Your Psychic Ability.* I would love to hear from you!

Facebook.com/MeetMattFraser
Twitter: @MeetMattFraser
Instagram: @MeetMattFraser

## Chapter 9 EXERCISE:

# *Putting Together Your Senses*

In this exercise you will learn how to use all of your senses to paint a picture of the question or situation you are dealing with in order to obtain guidance and also a solution.

First think of a situation or question that you need an answer for. Focus on the dilemma and follow the steps below, using your abilities to construct a mental image so that you may obtain an answer or guidance.

First turn to your intuition. What do you feel overall about the question or situation?

Turn to your clairvoyance. What do you see, or what symbols are being shown to you?

Next, turn to your clairsentience. What do you feel? What emotions arise regarding the question or situation?

Now let claircognizance have its turn: What initial thoughts come to mind?

What does clairaudience provide your hearing about the situation?

Lastly: Welcome the input of your angels and guides and ask them for comfort and guidance around the situation. How do they respond?

Do you see how easy everything flows and works together?

Once you have a better grasp of your psychic abilities, you will never be alone. Help will always be at your shoulder, ready to provide whatever assistance you require.

# KEYWORDS

**Spirit Guide:** A spirit who I assigned to you at birth to stand beside you and guide you as you walk through life.

**Clairvoyance:** The ability to see visions, symbols and mental pictures. Otherwise called clear seeing.

**Mediumship:** The ability to speak to those who have died and are in spirit.

**Clairsentience:** The ability to sense a situation or person through your emotions and feelings. Otherwise known as clear sensing.

**Claircognizant:** The ability to just know things about a person or situation without any prior knowledge. Otherwise known as clear knowing.

**Intuition:** An inner feeling or a sixth sense that allows you to feel a situation or question on a deeper level.

**Guardian Angel:** An angel that is assigned to you at birth that stands by you and projects you through life's obstacles.

**Psychic:** The ability to see, feel and sense the future through visions, symbols and hearing or through dreams.

**Clairaudience:** The ability to hear the future or hear those in spirit as opposed to seeing or feeling it.

**The Other Side:** A place beyond the veil where we enter after our soul leaves the physical world commonly referred to as heaven.

**Meditation:** A state of mind where you are completely relaxed, comfortable and in a sleep like state.

**White Light:** A protective energy often referred to as "The white light of Christ" used for protection and in meditation when connecting with the spiritual realm.

**Premonition Dreams:** The ability see or sense the future through dreams.

# ABOUT THE AUTHOR

Matt Fraser is America's Top Psychic Medium and star of the hit television series Meet The Frasers on E! Entertainment.

His sold-out live events, television appearances, and popular private readings have allowed him to bring healing, hope & laughter to a global audience of fans and followers from all around the world. From heartfelt emotional readings to stunning revelations, Matt Fraser has audiences on the edge of their seats with his outrageous personality and unique approach to mediumship.

His readings lead guests through a rollercoaster of emotions from laughing to crying, turning skeptics into believers with stunning details. His dynamic readings frequently include names, dates, and locations he couldn't possibly know, only adding to his long-established reputation. Matt's uncanny abilities and extreme accuracy have allowed him to reach millions world-wide from

A-list celebrities and influencers, to everyday people looking to get in touch with those they have lost.

A bestselling author and a psychic phenomenon, Matt has caught the attention of major media outlets across the nation including the New York Times, People magazine, and CBS Radio. He has also been a sought-after guest on popular TV shows such as The Real Housewives, Botched, The Doctors, and many more.

# CONTACT MATT FRASER:

Website: MeetMattFraser.com

**Call or Email:**

Phone: 401-573-1360
Email: Info@MeetMattFraser.com
Website: MeetMattFraser.com

**More ways to connect:**

Facebook.com/MeetMattFraser
Twitter: @MeetMattFraser
Instagram: @MeetMattFraser